What is a Union?
by Althea
illustrated by Chris Evans

© 1981 Rourke Enterprises, Inc.
© 1981 Althea Braithwaite
© 1981 Chris Evans, Illustrations

Published by Rourke Enterprises, Inc., P.O. Box 929, Windermere, Florida 32786. Copyright © 1981 by Rourke Enterprises, Inc. All copyrights reserved. No part of this book may be reproduced in any form without written permission from the publisher. Printed in the United States of America.

Library of Congress Cataloging in Publication Data

Althea.
  What is a union?

  Summary: Explains how trade unions function to make better working conditions for people.
    1. Trade-unions—Juvenile literature.
[1. Labor unions] I. Evans, Chris, ill.
II. Title.
HD6483.5.A42   1981   331.88   81-13800
ISBN 0-86592-570-4   AACR2

Rourke Enterprises, Inc.
Windermere, Florida 32786

The first trade unions were started about 200 years ago. They began because workers were not satisfied with working conditions. They had to work long hours in dark, dirty, dangerous places. They worked hard and were paid little money.

Some workers got the idea of joining together. In that way they would have more strength. They would ask for better working conditions and more pay. The factory owners might listen to a group.

Each group had a meeting and chose a spokesman. The spokesman would go and talk to the factory owners for them. These spokesmen have become known as shop stewards.

Today there are many different unions for people doing different kinds of jobs. Often there is more than one union in each factory.

In a factory making soft drinks there may be one union for the people who make the drink. Then, there is another union to look after the people printing the labels. Also, there is a third union for the people in the offices.

Some people think that unions spend all their time trying to get their members better pay and longer vacations or shorter hours.

In fact, they help in many other ways. They talk to the managers to make sure that the machines people use are safe. Unsafe machines can hurt people. Also, machines should not be too noisy. Very noisy machines can make people go deaf.

The union also helps arrange pensions. A pension ensures that people will still have money when they stop working. If a member is ill or has an accident the union sees that help is given.

Unions try to make sure there are jobs for everyone. This is a very difficult problem. One solution may be for people to work shorter hours. In this way more people are needed to keep the factory running.

People hope to work fewer hours, so they can spend more time at home with their families.

The unions also call meetings to talk about training programs. These programs help their members learn new jobs and work with new machinery. Unions also tell their members about new federal and state work laws.

People like to know about any changes that will be made and how the factory is doing.

Anyone in the factory might have a good idea to make things work better. The union can pass their ideas on to the management. The unions often give advice to help make the factory more successful. It is useful to have several points of view when deciding how to do things better.

At the soft drink factory the people making the drinks are upset. This is because one of the workers has been fired for not working fast enough.

The shop steward goes to the manager in charge and asks the managers to have a meeting about the problem. The worker says that something was wrong with the machine. That is why he was working slowly. After the meeting, the managers agree it was unfair to send the worker home.
He is rehired.
Everyone is pleased.

What if the managers had not rehired the worker? In that case the shop stewards would have called a union meeting to discuss what to do about it.

Sometimes, the union and the managers have very difficult problems. Even after much talking they cannot agree about what is fair for everyone.

If the union and the managers cannot agree, then the union may call a strike.

This means people in the union stop working. The factory has to close for a time, and the members do not get any pay. The factory has nothing to sell and no one is earning any money.

Everyone gets fed up and angry.
Unions usually do not like to strike.
However, sometimes it is the only way
to show managers how they feel.

Television, radio, and newspapers all report strikes. They talk about the number of working days lost by strikes.

Most people who belong to unions have never been on strike, and hope they will never have the need.

More working days
are lost by people being ill
than by people going on strike.

When factories are well run, the things they make will get sold. Then there is enough money to pay all the bills. The owners get good profits, the managers get good salaries and the workers get good pay and conditions.

Keeping everyone in the factory happy is not an easy task. There are different ideas about how to do it. Everyone hopes the factory can be made a good place in which to work. Everyone hopes they can have enough money to live comfortably and enjoy life.